*Great Artists
of the World*

Vincent
van Gogh

Alix Wood

W
FRANKLIN WATTS
LONDON•SYDNEY

Franklin Watts

First published in Great Britain in 2015 by the Watts Publishing Group

Copyright © Alix Wood Books
Produced for Franklin Watts by Alix Wood Books www.alixwoodbooks.co.uk

Editor: Eloise Macgregor
Designer: Alix Wood

Photo Credits: Cover, 1, 21 © Peter Willi - Artothek; 4 top © ARC; 7 © nga;
9 © Imagno - Artothek; 10 © Jean-Pol Grandmont; 13 © Peter Willi - Artothek;
15 © Blauel/Gnamm - Artothek; 17 © Peter Willi - Artothek; 19 © Christie's
Images Ltd - Artothek ; 22-23 © Hans Hinz - Artothek; 25 © Hans Hinz - Artothek;
26-27 © Artothek; 27 top © Francisco J. Gonzalez; 29 left © philophoto/Shutterstock;
3, 4 bottom, 8, 11, 28, 29 right © Shutterstock

Dewey number 709

ISBN 978 1 4451 4413 9

Library eBook ISBN 978 1 4451 4414 6

Printed in China

Franklin Watts
An imprint of
Hachette Children's Group
Part of The Watts Publishing Group
Carmelite House
50 Victoria Embankment
London EC4Y 0DZ

An Hachette UK Company

www.hachette.co.uk

www.franklinwatts.co.uk

Contents

Who Was Vincent van Gogh?

Vincent Willem van Gogh was born on March 30, 1853 in Groot-Zundert, a village near Breda in the Netherlands. He was the oldest child of Theodorus van Gogh, a minister of the Dutch Reformed Church, and Anna Cornelia Carbentus. Vincent was a painter who became well known for his bold colours and his swirly style of painting.

Vincent van Gogh

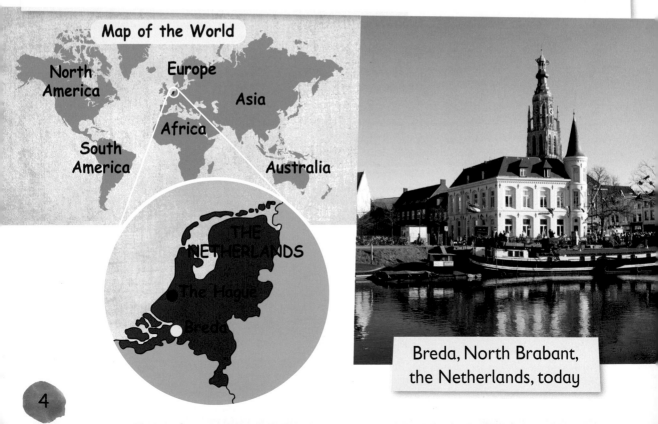

Map of the World

North America

Europe

Asia

Africa

South America

Australia

THE NETHERLANDS

The Hague

Breda

Breda, North Brabant, the Netherlands, today

Vincent was close to his younger brother Theo. He also had another brother and three sisters. Vincent was a serious, quiet child. He went to the local village school, where one teacher taught around 200 pupils! After a year, he and his sister Anna were taught at home by a **governess**, until he went to boarding school at Zevenbergen about 20 miles (32 km) away. He was sad to leave his family. At 13 Vincent went to college, but left suddenly at 15 without graduating.

Vincent's brother, Theo

Vincent's Art

Vincent began to draw as a child, but he did not begin painting until his late twenties. Then he made up for lost time! In just over ten years, he painted 860 oil paintings and more than 1,300 watercolours, drawings, sketches and prints! He is best known for his **self portraits**, and his landscapes of cypress trees, wheat fields and sunflowers.

Sunflowers in a field in France

Vincent's First Jobs

Vincent's first job was working for the firm of **art dealers**, Goupil & Cie. His uncle Vincent, whom he called "Uncle Cent" helped him get the job. After training in The Hague, in the Netherlands, he moved to a branch in London, England. This was a happy time for Vincent. He was successful and was, at 20, earning more than his father. Vincent then moved to the main branch in Paris, France.

Goupil & Cie in Paris

Vincent began to dislike art being treated as a thing to buy and sell. Customers sensed his dislike, which wasn't good for business. In the end, his boss fired him. Vincent returned to England and taught at a boarding school. He then worked in a bookstore in the Netherlands for six months. Unhappy, he spent his time doodling or translating the Bible into English, French and German.

Vincent decided to follow his father and become a **minister**. His parents agreed to pay for his education, but Vincent started work as a minister with the coal miners of Borinage, a poor area of Belgium. He liked the miners, their lifestyle and their families. After working in Borinage for a while, his brother Theo persuaded him to use his artistic talent, and become an artist instead.

The Potato Eaters, 1885. When Vincent painted in later years, he remembered the working people of Borinage.

Letters to Theo

Vincent missed his brother Theo when they were apart. The two wrote to each other often. They exchanged hundreds of letters between 1872 and 1890, with more than 600 from Vincent to Theo and 40 from Theo to Vincent. The only gap was a time when Vincent lived in Paris, because the brothers lived together and had no need to write!

Vincent sketched pictures in his letters, and often wrote notes all around the edge of the paper. With so many letters going to and from Vincent's house, it's not surprising he got to know a postman very well! He was good friends with postman Joseph Roulin (right), and painted several portraits of his whole family. Vincent's letters were very interesting. In them he described what he was painting, and often did little drawings of his work to show Theo what they looked like.

Portrait of Joseph Roulin, 1889.

Choosing Art

Vincent moved to Cuesmes, in Belgium. His interest in being a minister began to fade. He decided to become an artist instead. Theo helped Vincent by sending money, and Vincent took some lessons at an art academy in Brussels.

The house where Van Gogh stayed in Cuesmes in 1880, when he decided to become an artist

No, Nay, Never

In April 1881, Vincent moved to the countryside near Breda with his family. He continued drawing, often using neighbours as models. He spent time walking and talking with his cousin, Kee Vos-Stricker. He asked her to marry him, but she said no. In fact, she said, "No, nay, never!" Kee's father wouldn't let Vincent see her and this upset him. That Christmas Vincent refused to go to church, argued with his father and left home for The Hague.

In The Hague, Vincent spent time with Anton Mauve, a relative, who was a painter. Mauve lent him money to set up a **studio**. The two soon had a disagreement and stopped speaking, though.

Restless, Vincent moved to his parent's new home in Nuenen. He liked to paint weavers at work. His neighbour Margot Begemann sometimes went painting with him. They wanted to marry, but their families were against it.

Vincent started getting interest in Paris for his work. He also showed paintings in the window of a paint dealer in The Hague. During the next two years he did nearly 200 oil paintings! His **palette** was very dark, nothing like the bright paintings he is famous for. When he complained that Theo was not trying hard enough to sell his work in Paris, his brother wrote back telling him his paintings were too dark and unfashionable.

Vincent's first paintings used very dark colours.

11

Antwerp and Paris

In 1885, Vincent moved to Antwerp, Belgium. He had little money and hardly ate, spending the money Theo sent on painting materials and models. He went to the Academy of Fine Arts to study painting. He visited museums where he admired the bright new painting styles. He began to add brighter colours to his work.

Vincent moved to Paris in March 1886 to live with Theo, and studied at Fernand Cormon's studio. He met many talented artists there. His friends included Paul Signac, Emile Bernard, Henri de Toulouse-Lautrec, Camille Pissarro, John Peter Russell, and later, Paul Gauguin.

Père Tanguy's Shop

Julien Tanguy ran an art supply shop in Paris. His happy nature and love of art made his shop popular, and he was nicknamed "père" or "father" Tanguy. He shared his food and money with struggling artists and happily exhibited their paintings. Tanguy would take paintings as payment for paints, so his shop was a colourful gallery!

Portrait of Père Tanguy, 1887. Vincent decorated the walls of his studio with Japanese woodblock prints. You can see them in the background of this painting.

13

A House in Arles

Vincent moved to Arles, in southern France. He stayed in hotels first, and then rented the Yellow House. He had a dream of starting an artists' **colony**. He made friends with US artist Dodge MacKnight and Danish artist Christian Mourier-Petersen. Vincent painted some of his best works in Arles. He was very busy.

This is what he painted in one month, September 1888

The Café Terrace at Night
The Entrance to the Public Park in Arles
The Green Vineyard
A Lane in the Public Garden at Arles
Night Café in the Place Lamartine in Arles
The Old Mill
Ploughed Field
Portrait of Eugène Boch
The Poet's Garden
The Self-Portrait (Dedicated to Paul Gauguin)
The Sower: Outskirts of Arles in the Background
Starry Night Over the Rhone
Vincent's House in Arles (The Yellow House)
Portrait of Milliet, Second Lieutenant of the Zouaves

That's about two days per masterpiece!

Unsigned

Vincent didn't sign the *Café Terrace* painting (right). We know it was by him as he described it in a letter to his sister. He painted it on the spot, instead of in his studio. He had trouble telling the paints apart in the dark though! This is the first painting he did with his famous starry background.

The Café Terrace at Night, 1888

Bedroom in Arles

Vincent painted his bedroom in the Yellow House three times. The painting on the right was the third version, a small copy done for his mother and sister. The portraits on the wall are believed to be the portraits of his friends Eugène Boch and Paul-Eugène Milliet. The one above the bed is unknown. It may be by someone else or it may be a missing work.

Vincent doesn't seem to have many things in his bedroom. Neither of the doors are a cupboard. The door on the right went to the staircase, and the door to the left led to the guest room. His clothes and hat are hanging up on pegs. You can see a bowl and jug of water on the table ready for him to wash.

It looks at first like Vincent has painted the back wall wrong, but he hasn't. The room was an odd shape and had an angled back wall. Vincent often painted chairs like the ones in the painting.

Bedroom in Arles, 1889

Draw Your Bedroom

What would you put in a drawing of your bedroom? Will it look as tidy as Vincent's? We can guess from this painting that Vincent really liked his bedroom. His bed looks comfortable and he has all his favourite paintings around him.

A Visit from Gauguin

Vincent first met artist Paul Gauguin in Paris when Vincent had organised an art exhibition. After seeing the exhibition Gauguin arranged to swap one of his paintings for two of Vincent's sunflowers studies. When Gauguin agreed to visit Arles, Vincent hoped he would stay and help create his dream of an artist's colony.

Paul Gauguin

Vincent was very excited. He painted sunflowers to decorate Gauguin's room. Gauguin finally arrived and for two months the two lived and painted together. They visited galleries together, and Gauguin painted Vincent's portrait. After a while, their friendship began to turn sour. Vincent admired Gauguin and wanted to be treated as his equal, but Gauguin was **arrogant**. They argued a lot about art.

Fourteen Sunflowers in a Vase, 1889.

The Argument and the Ear

One evening Vincent and Gauguin had an argument. Gauguin claimed Vincent threatened him with a knife. It has long been believed that later that evening Vincent went home and cut off a good part of his left ear. He then wrapped the ear in cloth and gave it as a present to a woman he knew. The police were called and Vincent was taken to the hospital.

Did Gauguin Do It?

Some think Vincent made up the story to protect Gauguin, who actually cut Vincent's ear off during the argument. Both men kept silent, Gauguin to avoid arrest and Vincent in an attempt to keep his valued friend. Gauguin was an excellent swordsman. He wanted to leave Arles, and perhaps walked out of the house with his cases and sword in his hand, but was followed by the upset Vincent. It is possible they fought, and Gauguin cut off Vincent's left earlobe, either in anger or self-defence.

Self-portrait, 1889. This was painted not long after Vincent cut off his left ear. Why can you see his left ear in this picture? Vincent painted self-portraits by looking in a mirror, so this is really his right ear.

The Asylum

Vincent returned home but spent the next month going in and out of hospital suffering from **hallucinations** and thinking he was being poisoned. In March 1889, 30 people from Arles wrote to ask the police to close his house so Vincent couldn't return. They called him the "fou roux" (the redheaded madman).

By May, still struggling with his mental health, Vincent decided to go into an **asylum**. He was thought to have a type of **epilepsy**. The asylum was surrounded by cornfields, vineyards and olive trees. Theo arranged for two cells next to each other for Vincent, so that one could be used as a studio. As long as he remained stable, the doctors let Vincent paint. He did 150 paintings during his stay.

The Hospital at Arles, 1889. Vincent was stopped from painting after he tried to eat his paint during one attack. After a while, the doctors let him paint again.

The Starry Night

The Starry Night is probably Vincent van Gogh's best known painting. The painting is of the view outside his window at the asylum. Unusually for Vincent, it was painted from memory during the day. Perhaps that is how he got so much feeling into the painting.

Vincent used thick brush strokes and often used paint straight out of the tube. He laid down each stroke of colour carefully and separately. His style was influenced by an **Impressionist** style called *pointillism* where dots of primary colours are put on the canvas and our eyes mix them to create other colours. Vincent used strokes instead, using the direction, length and curve to get the look he wanted. The twirling sky is full of curving, short brush strokes. The peaceful buildings have straight, longer lines.

Here is an example of how pointillism works. Only dots of the three primary colours, red, blue and yellow, have been used. Where the dots of yellow and blue are close to each other, your eyes mix the colour so it looks green.

The Starry Night, 1889

Happy or Sad Painting?

What do you think? The village is dark and the swirly clouds in the night sky could seem frightening. The brightly lit windows in the village make it look homely and friendly, though, and the church in the middle might be protecting the houses.

Vincent's Last Days

When Vincent left the asylum he moved to Auvers-sur-Oise, near Paris, to be close to his doctor and to Theo. During the two months between his arrival, on 21 May, and his death on 29 July, Vincent did about 70 paintings. That's more than one a day!

On July 27, Vincent shot himself in the chest with a revolver. Where he was when he shot himself is unclear, perhaps the wheatfield or at a barn near the inn where he was staying. He managed to get back to the inn, the Auberge Ravoux, and two doctors were called. They couldn't remove the bullet. The following morning Theo rushed to be with Vincent. At first it seemed as if he would get better, but he died in the evening of an infection in the wound.

Vincent died in a room on the top floor of the Auberge Ravoux (right). When asked if he had meant to kill himself, he apparently replied "Yes I believe so." Some think he was shot by a teenage boy who used to buy him drinks and tease him. His easel and brushes that he had taken with him that day were never found. Neither were a suicide note or a gun.

Wheatfield with Crows, 1890
This was one of Vincent's last paintings.

Vincent's Legacy

A legacy is what is left behind when someone dies. Usually it is money, or things that the person owned, to be inherited by their children. Vincent wrote in a letter to Theo that, as he did not have any children, he saw his paintings as his children.

Van Gogh's new approach to painting had a strong influence on the next generation of artists. His use of unusual colours, angular heavy lines and obvious brushstrokes and patterns influenced many artists that followed. His **distortion** of reality also inspired artists that came after him.

Vincent's Grave

Vincent was buried the day after he died in the cemetery behind the church at Auvers-sur-Oise. Theo died the following year from a mixture of illness and grief at the loss of his brother. The two were eventually buried side by side.

ICI REPOSE
VINCENT van GOGH
1853 1890

FRANCE POSTES 1979

A French stamp with Vincent's painting *The Church at Auvers-sur-Oise*, 1890

VINCENT VAN GOGH
L'EGLISE D'AUVERS SUR OISE

A photo of the same church

You can see that the church in the painting is the same church as the one in the photograph. The difference is the painting gives the church a character and atmosphere that the photo does not. That is what Vincent made his paintings do. In a letter to Theo, Vincent said "real painters do not paint things as they are. They paint them as they themselves feel them to be". That ability is Vincent's legacy that he leaves behind for us all.

Glossary

arrogant
Overly proud of oneself or one's own opinions.

art dealers
People or companies that buy and sell works of art.

asylum
An institution for the care of those unable to care for themselves and especially for the insane.

colony
A group of people with common interests who live close to each other.

distortion
The condition of being twisted out of a natural, normal or original shape.

epilepsy
A disorder causing convulsions and loss of consciousness.

governess
A woman who teaches and trains a child in a private home.

hallucinations
Seeing things that are not really there.

Impressionist

An artist who concentrates on the impression of a scene using unmixed primary colours and small brush strokes to simulate light.

minister

One who performs religious ceremonies in church services.

palette

A board used by a painter to mix paints on.

self-portraits

Paintings of oneself made by oneself.

studio

The working place of an artist.

Websites

Metropolitan Museum of Art site with facts about Van Gogh
http://www.metmuseum.org/metmedia/kids-zone/art-trek/how-van-gogh-made-his-mark

BBC bitesize video about Van Gogh's life
http://www.bbc.co.uk/education/clips/z4pvcdm

Read More

Mayhew, James. *Katie and the Starry Night*. London, UK: Orchard Books, 2013.

Venezia, Mike. *Vincent Van Gogh* (Getting to Know the World's Greatest Artists) revised edition. London, UK: Franklin Watts, 2014.

Zaczek, Iain. *In the Picture With: Vincent Van Gogh*. London, UK: Wayland, 2014.

Index